When Was the Last Time

Amitesh Ranjan

Clever Fox®
PUBLISHING

Chennai • Bangalore

CLEVER FOX PUBLISHING
Chennai, India

Published by CLEVER FOX PUBLISHING 2025

ISBN: 978-93-6707-056-7

This is a work of fiction and is based upon the imagination of the authors.

Any resemblance to any living and dead would purely be coincidental.

All the opinions expressed in this book are solely of the authors and have no intent to hurt the sentiment of any person or faith or belief. If this still affects anyone, I apologizeto them in advance.

Contents

Dedicated to My Son Shreeyansh -

- the best teacher of my life.

Prelude

Learning is an everyday thing. It does not require any specific situation, place, time, or designation to learn. The only precursor of learning is openness and a willingness to learn.

This book is a learning documentary of my experiences over last 20 years of work. These learning experiences has cropped up while working across the geography of India, spreading through 3 companies I worked with, and more than 25 states and 200 cities I travelled to.

Some learning has deep knowledge; some is just everyday learning. All these helped me build my character and personality.

Most of the learning that is mentioned here has the starting point with the phrase "When Was The Last Time…". So have used this phrase as the documentary heading and have drafted it in a way to make it a complete story.

Each topic has some context, reflection, and my ways of doing things. The way could be different for different individuals, and is just a guardrail to think towards this.

Most of the time, when a certain situation came to me, it was a choice to think straight and be conventional or think laterally to stem a different solution. Not all the time did I succeed to solve the situation, but I have got a good life learning every time. These learnings are like a lighthouse for me and always help me to get a right direction when I get into a tough situation.

A popular saying is that, best learning comes by making mistakes, just to keep in mind that the mistake should not be repeated. I think repeating the mistake is very common since it's not every time that we get into identical situations. The catch is, reducing the occurrence of these mistakes. Solving this will decide how successful we are. Most of the great leaders make mistakes; the only difference between them and others is their quantum of mistakes.

The topics selected in this book are the everyday things and are not essentially a Eureka topic that will fix all life problems. It now depends upon the readers on how they are interpreting this in their everyday lives.

Let's try moving towards becoming individuals open for learning, not waiting for a big event to lead to the learning, but to find opportunities for learning every day, every moment, and in every situation.

Happy Reading

Amitesh Ranjan

Acknowledgement

This book is the learning compilation from many leaders I worked with, many situations I came across, and many teams I led in different organizations and tenures. Acknowledging few may be injustice to many. But since it is mandatory to mention some names to acknowledge, here are a few without neglecting the importance of many teachers in my life.

I would like to extend thanks to **Mr K P Babu**, **Mr Jagdeesh Sontakke**, **Mr Balasubramaniam TR,** who were a few of my early LMs and teachers for extending their experience and giving me a great learning.

I would like to thank **Vinay Vishwakarma**, **Akhil Agarwal**, **Vikram Garga**, **Siddarth Menon**, **Deepak Agarwal**, **Ganesh Ramani**, **Dr Jiyaul Hoque**, **Ambarish Sikarwar**, **Adyan Prabhakaran** and **Nitin Jain** who were my LM, LM2 and senior during different organizations and different roles I was in. These leaders taught me the right way of thinking. They also taught me what not to do. I learned from their successes and, at times, their failures as well.

Would like to extend my thanks to **Gyan Prakash**, **Gaurav Tilekar**, **Gaurav Garg**, **Dr Kiran Kasid**, **Zena Chatwal**, **Abhishek Khatri**, **Dr Ganga Singh Shekhawat**, **Govind Chandran**, **Dr Sandeep Bidre**, **Avik Sengupta**, **Dr Sukumar Chand**, **Suhas LS**, **Gajendra Patel,** with whom I worked and have been friends forever . These were the constant source of my motivation during different phases of the professional journey. Their experiences have taught me a lot. A few of the topics are taken from their experiences that I found helpful for me.

Most importantly, my parents, my siblings, and immediate family were the constant source of energy in my different thick and thin times of life.

Above all is **Lord Mahakaal**, who is my one and only source of energy; who was always there with me in every situation, time and state of mind

About the Author

Amitesh Ranjan is one of the billion people on Earth who believe in a simple life and living the way he wants to live, without affecting anyone negatively.

He is a middle-level leader and has worked with different great organizations where his capabilities were best improved and best utilized.

Amitesh has been into active writing since 2000 when he started working with a leading newspaper as a part-time job. He has authored many blogs, short stories – both in Hindi and English, short travelogues and, Hindi poetry.

He is the author of 4 titles available on all the major D-com portals.

His first book was **"Baked Thoughts"**. This is the collection of his blogs he wrote in the first 10 years of his professional career.

His 2nd book is **"Kinche",** which he wrote in Hindi. This is a collection of short stories and is well appreciated by many.

He wrote his 3rd book with his son, Shreeyansh. The title of the book is **"The Adventures of Ricky"**. This is the collection of extempore stories which he and his son had created during bedtime. This book has very good reviews and a reader group. This book is very close to the author's heart as this was created by his then 5-years-old son.

His 4th book was again a short story collection in Hindi. The title of the book is **"Narmada Nandlaal"**. This book has stories that he observed in every people he met or came across. This was featured in the 2 consecutive World Book Fair, Delhi and was able to attract conscious readers to pick this book.

"When Was The Last Time" is the 5th book in a row and is a collection of the documentary of his learning during his corporate career spanning around 20 years.

He is working on a few other projects that will see the light of day soon.

Forward

I have had the opportunity of working with Amitesh for around ten years as part of a memorable journey we traversed in the Petcare category. I have seen him grow in every sense of the word from where he was to where he is now. One thing that remained constant was his keen desire to learn. Even when things were tough and seemingly insurmountable, he was always open to learn with refreshing vulnerability.

His leadership journey has also been truly remarkable. In every role, he has been able to nurture and groom his team, see them grow, and take bigger roles within and outside the organisation. His solution mindset, coming from his ability to draw from his collective experience and thereby guiding his team, has been exemplary.

I remember once I could not resist asking him about how he could devote time seamlessly to each of his roles of a Sales leader, a passionate writer, a doting father and so much more…? He said in a nonchalant manner, **"I have a date with myself every week".** Lesson learnt for me. His ability to compartmentalise time for multiple priorities of life allowed for his multidimensional growth as a person.

When I went through the book, I could ascertain that every section has come out of his personal experience and that of people around him. In his inimitable lucid style, he has brought to life a distilled version of learnings which can be easily understood and practiced.

This book is a must-read for anyone and everyone who wants to push their mental barriers, broaden their horizons, and develop themselves holistically. It will serve as a ready reckoner for finding a way out whenever you get stuck in your career or even in your personal life.

I wish Amitesh loads of success in his journey ahead, and waiting for many more books to his credit.

Happy Reading!

Nitin Jain

Chief Operating Officer
Godrej Pet Care Limited

JUMP OVER THE BOUNDARY

When was the last time you jumped over the boundary?

When things start going in the direction of our desire, we become complacent over time and start believing that "I know because I mastered".

I was having a conversation with one of the members of the Leadership Team of our organization, and this question was thrown to me by him.

This was a very strong line that put me into brooding. Is it that I had created a boundary around me and didn't want to come out of that? Is it that complacency plays a major role in putting me into my comfort zone? Am I getting into indolence while everything around me is flowing fast?

> *Complacency plays a major role in putting us into a comfort zone.*

We work hard to make our place in our spaces – be it personal or professional. Once we reach a level that we thought of, if not fancied, we start making it our credited space. We start believing that we have arrived, and that is the point when we actually start getting into the comfort zone. We start building our own invisible boundary, defining our territory. We become so used to of the space that we start believing that the world outside our boundary is of no use to us since our space is a better space, built over solid works and invested in time. At times, we don't even try peeping out of the boundary to at least understand the outside world.

If you have such traits, or see these traits, then perhaps you are becoming superfluous for the space you are in. There is a risk of becoming irrelevant in space and may reach the obsolete level.

I think it is very much required that we should be dynamic enough to be best suited in a changing environment. We should be courageous enough to jump over the boundary we have perhaps built ourselves.

Most of the popular failure stories are a result of the same invisible boundary and resistance to jumping over it. My view is that failure happens because someone is reluctant to jump over the boundary, because someone believes that "I know because I mastered" without knowing the fact that what they mastered is obsolete now in the current dynamic environment.

> *Most of the popular failure stories are result of resistance to jump over the boundary of complacency.*

A few of the quick steps to not fall prey to this are: -

1. **Embrace Changes** – This is a perpetual truth that we all need to accept. Change is inevitable and will happen, whether we like it or not. What is important and crucial is whether we are open to change and ready to embrace it. Getting into the nostalgia of "during our days" is absolutely fine, but it doesn't mean that we should stop acknowledging the change and continue living in the good old days. Chances are that we will become a past if we continue living in the past and be in denial of change.
2. **Be Agile** – We must be agile to the changing environment. You cannot eliminate change, but change can eliminate you otherwise. Let's adjust ourselves according to the changing needs and be ready to adapt to the situation. After all we are designed for adaptation. Darwin's theory has made us realize that we did not originate as humans on Earth but had adapted to become one. So just take note of it and show agility.
3. **Be Future Ready** – Invest in your own development every 5 years. This will enable you to be future ready. Many of the great leaders believe that investing in

ourselves is the best investment and can never be denigrated. My father was always pushing us to be future ready by investing 10% of the yearly income in self-development. Be it joining some skill upgradation courses, workshops, online courses, or acquiring new learning that is relevant to the changing environment.

4. **Read Every Day** – This is one of the ways to keep you charged and updated. Read whatever you like; reading is important. I feel that reading has nothing to do with a penchant or an aversion. Everyone must read whatever topic is required to be understood. Read to learn new things, read to refresh yourself, read to upgrade, but read. Reading is the most common thing among almost all the business leaders we know. Even if they are quite busy, they take some time out to read books. There is no very specific time for reading. Read whenever you have time. This will always help.

So next time when you feel conquering your space, ask yourselves – **"When was the last time you jumped over the boundary?"**

A DATE WITH YOURSELVES : ME TIME

When was the last time you had a date with yourself?

We live life in a pie to make the circle of our life. While these are kind of fixed pie, getting any adjustment in that makes us compromise with the other part. In all these adjustments, we miss having a part for ourselves. And that's where the entire issue arises.

I think a "ME" time is need of hour in the current intricate lifestyle. This could be a big enabler to live a stress-free life. In the current generation, there is a lot to do in life, and it is leaving literally no time for us.

We should always practice carving out "ME" time out of our daily schedules. Mostly, this ME time should be utilized by us to organize our thoughts, retrospect, introspect, and follow our passion.

> Follow simple "Early to Bed and Early to Rise" phrase strictly. This will unlock many hours of your life.

Most of the time, we hear complaints that it is difficult to take time out of the current busy schedule. Yes, absolutely right, but it all depends on how we see time.

Is 24 hours too less or that we have 24 hours every day, should be the question we should ask ourselves.

One easy way of taking some time out from these fixed 24 hours is following easy discipline in life. Means we should be strict on sleeping and waking up times every day. If it is difficult to sleep early, at least give some tasks to your alarm clock. Wake up early. Follow this for a few days, and you would realize that your body's biological clock adjusts accordingly and would start sending signals to sleep early. If we could be able to manage this for 2 weeks, we would find a few hours more in our life every day. If it is just an hour that you could manage with this, that counts as 7 hours per week! Is this not something that was there with you and you have not unlocked so far? Now it's up to you how you use these 7 hours for yourselves.

I think if we manage an hour every day for ourselves, it will help us a lot in following our passion, organizing our thoughts to be more effective, and give time to our health by doing some workout like cycling, swimming, running, or yoga. Or like me, if you have the hobby of writing, you can write a blog, a poem, or even plot to write something big. I follow this strictly and save 2 hours almost every day, which has resulted in authoring 4 books, numerous blogs, articles, stories, and poems. All of these was done while working in an active and time demanding job, without compromising on it. This saved time has helped me read books almost every day for 30 – 35 minutes. Not that you would always feel like doing some or the other thing with these times. Just being in silence and not thinking about anything is also doing something and making time productive. This will help you have a better connection with yourself. Being with ourselves is very much required. We should learn to talk to ourselves and must know what to talk about and how to talk to ourselves. Spend time talking to yourself.

> *Take out 3 hours a week for yourself and do something that your heart follows.*

I generally try taking an hour out of my daily schedule to be with myself. I take my cycle and ride to a park near my house. It is around 4 KM from my house. I sit there quietly, talk to myself, understand what I did yesterday and what I will have to do today and for the next few days, plan accordingly, and take a commitment from myself of ensuring to do that basis the self-talking. Sounds weird, let it be. As long as I feel it works for me, I don't care what others are thinking.

> Saved time should not be waisted by procrastinating.

In this quest of saving time and spending it for us, the only catch is you are saving time to utilize in productive ways than spending further on something not very meaningful, like watching mobile or playing video games. Not that these are total waste. But if all the time saved by us is spent on these gaming or binge watching on mobile, then we are actually not intentional about utilizing it in knowing ourselves or doing something that could be different from trivial things, and actually not intentional towards doing something for ourselves.

Do take time out for yourself, if not an hour per day, at least 3 hours per week. You can feel the difference once you start having ME time. Having a date with ourselves is a good idea.

So next time, you are feeling low, ask yourself, **"When was the last time you had a date with yourself?"**.

AGREE TO DISAGREE

When was the last time you agreed upon someone's disagreement?

Most of the time, we keep our views straight. We agree or we disagree. But not often do we agree to disagree.

This would sound a bit complex, but it is a much easier term.

When things fit in with our experience or understanding, or belief, we do not take time to agree. A vice-versa situation leads to disagreement.

A bit lateral view is, when we agree on terms or thoughts, it leads to a roadblock situation, and can seldom lead to creating something new or going beyond our belief. It can be a fulfilling status that we refuse to create new. While agreement can lead to closure of the task, it is also the culmination for the thoughts.

While in other situations of disagreement, if not on the same page, it could lead to an argumentative situation and even turn to stress if not handled well.

> *Experiences can be totally different for different individuals in the same situation.*

Taking the difference of opinion prudently is an art. Different people can have different opinions about the same situation or happening, as opinions are made based on our individual experiences. The experiences can be totally different for different individuals in the same situation. The ways of seeing things can be different for different individuals. We cannot expect everyone to have exactly the same opinion every time in the same situation. In fact, we must understand that similar opinions happen only for the universal truth, occurrence, or phenomenon. Most often we try changing the opinion of people as per our comfort, and that leads to a very contrite situation, in turn leading to stress or differences. We must understand that thoughts cannot always be twining. While having a healthy disagreement is absolutely fine, we must understand that there is an invisible line drawn between disagreement and the quest to make people come to an agreement.

> *Taking the difference of opinion prudently is an art.*

Disagreement, according to me, brings better opinions, varied opinions, and gives us more space to take quality decisions. The only thing is giving space to disagreement and taking it sportingly without being judgmental or opinionated.

Handling disagreement is an art, and mastering it is not a big task. Here are some of the pointers that we can practice to handle disagreement: -

1. **Listening:** This is very important as most of the time disagreement happens because we do not listen actively. When we are in a conversation where the objective is to bring agreement, it is important to listen without interrupting the other person. We should raise questions only once the other person finishes their dialogue. This will not only give space to the person to explain things but also give us time to process the information shared before getting into the hurry of answering or debating.
2. **Openness:** Being open in any negotiation conversation helps bring consensus or agreement. While getting into such a conversation, we must listen with open minds rather than being preoccupied. This is one of the best ways to bring agreement or win the negotiation. If we are in a discussion with our own assumptions, and not guided by the data or facts, it will never lead to an amicable ending.
3. **Clear and Pragmatic Goals:** When we want to bring agreement upon something, it is important that we

have a clear outcome expectation and that it must be realistic. If we are in conversation with our team and want to bring growth for the business with an expectation of 5x achievement over the average, we will have to go to the drawing board to understand if this is a realistic task, and whether we are ever going to reach an agreement over this with the team. If we still feel 5x is possible, we must put the reasons with data and logic, and support to bring that achievement.

4. **Find Common Ground:** An agreement many times can be made on the condition of our own set goals or process. We need to be flexible enough to find a common ground and be ready to travel to that ground.
5. **Respectful:** While getting into a negotiation discussion, when things are not looking like they are going in the right direction, we tend to move towards being sarcastic with the other side or start sounding harsh or tough. I think being respectful is very important in any case. Whether we are moving towards a disagreement or agreement, it is important to handle people with respect and try to win with logic rather than an attitude.

It is important to practice taking disagreement gracefully and agreeing to the disagreement. A disagreement will definitely bring a bigger and better outcome for sure. If not, it will surely bring a good experience.

So next time when it feels like bringing someone to your agreement, ask yourself, **"When was the last time you agreed to disagree?"**.

AN EYE FOR LOVE

When was the last time you saw love through the eyes of your heart?

There is a popular saying, "Beauty lies in the eyes of beholder". I had a slightly protracted learning that "Love could be felt with eyes first". Throughout my career, I have worked with core FMCG organizations and have mechanically worked towards distribution, dealing with the channel partners and people.

When I was changing the organization in 2013, I was a little apprehensive for the company as this organization wasn't a typical FMCG company. I appeared in all the rounds of their assessment and passed in all. It was the last HR round with the HR Manager. It was merely a formality before the offer letters, and something very drastic may not happen. The HR Manager asked me, "Do you love Dogs?"

"Umm, not really. However, I don't hate them either", was my plain reply. It was a spontaneous answer that I hadn't realized that this could cost me the job. After all I was appearing for an interview for a Pet Food Company.

The HR lady was impassive. She said, "What do you do when you see stray dogs while going back home in the evening?"

What kind of question is this? I have never observed that they exist even. I drive back home mostly in my car or at times in a taxi. But yes, whenever I am walking nearby stores for some top-up grocery needs, at times they woof, and it scares me a lot.

"When I get petrified, I try scooting them away with whatever is there in my hand. Some of the times I even have picked stones from the road and thrown at them to scare them." I don't know why I kept doing a self-goal by responding this way to her.

"Hmm, so what I heard is that you throw stones at them if you get scared, she rephrased, Amitesh, today, when you go back home, I would recommend buying a packet of biscuits and when they bark at you, throw some biscuits at them. You will see the magic." With this advice, she got into completing the formalities of the employment.

I landed in Kolkata at around 10 in the evening. I took a radio cab and was on the way home. While in the taxi, I was reviewing the entire day and trying to comprehend if the day was productive for me or not. I don't know, for some reason, I asked my cab driver to stop at a shop for a while. I went inside and looked for pet food. I did not find it. I bought a couple of packs of Parle Biscuit and came back to the taxi. I was just having a laptop bag with me. So, I stopped the cab around half a kilometre before my society. I came out of the taxi and walked towards my apartment.

> *How much tolerant we could be that just by a small gesture of love, we can forget all the past transgressions.*

There were 4 – 5 strays on the way back. I got a piece of advice today on what to do when a stray dog barks. I took the biscuit packet out of my bag and gave a couple of it to the nearest dog. It suddenly stopped barking and ate it fast. After finishing, that dog upstretched its head to look towards me. That was the first day when I actually had eye contact with any dog. The light over the street was a bit dim coming from that 20-feet-tall streetlight. In that dim light, I saw into that dog's eye. Oh my God. That dog's eye was filled with love and compassion towards me. Just by having a few biscuits, that dog literally forgot and exonerated all my shooing and stones that I would have thrown at them. How much tolerant we could be that just by a small gesture of love, can forget all the past transgressions. They are. This beautiful dog took a piece of my heart immediately. I literally fell in love with this mighty creature. Had that HR manager not told me to do so, I would never have bought the biscuits for them and would not have gained this beautiful experience.

Ever since, I had seen nothing but love for me in their eyes. They keep getting pet food from me now, but that is just a small token of love from my side for the immense love they are showering over me.

So, whenever you see a free wandering animal, ask yourself, **"When was the last time you saw love through the eyes of your heart?"**

If not, let's show some love for them, you will get n^{th} times more love in return. This is our social responsibility too to take care of our ecosystem. They are part of our ecosystem and must get care in return from all of us.

#BREAKTHEBIAS – LET'S START FROM HOME

When was the last time you took efforts to break the bias at home?

There happen to be a time when Doordarshan was playing a government ad on female feticide and its legal consequences. The then Indian Society was paranoid about having a male kid those days. Now majority of India (unfortunately, not the entire India yet) has accepted the fact that for having a kid, gender doesn't matter. The shift had been visible when Gen X and Gen Y became decision makers to a larger extent. With the accent of Millennials, the society has started showing even more openness towards this.

But the bias is still there.

> *We are programmed to think patriarchal.*

While acceptance towards girl children has increased, there is still a stereotype working. Still, while deciding the work, a diversity of physical capabilities is being considered. Various other factors are also playing a decisive role in deciding the job level for female employees. For instance, when I had to recruit an Area Sales Manager for Punjab, I asked our HR to source CVs of diverse candidates (diversity in India is still at a very nascent stage where it simply means gender diversity and that too with only two genders mostly). Our HR had a different set of problems that were beyond her control. In a discussion, our HR Manager said that most of the organizations are targeting "diverse candidates" to improve the gender imbalance. This had led to a demand: supply constraint. A sales job is still not an opted profession by the majority of female candidates, and hence, the current situation will continue.

There are many such professions/branches where ladies of India do not opt as an obvious choice for their career and, hence any organization would face trouble in driving #breakthebias trend, irrespective of how much intentional they are. Just imagine any organization asking for a civil engineer, factory apprentice, or even a CA. There is a gap between demand and supply. The sales professional is definitely a constrained department for diversity.

> *#breakthebias trend, I feel, is the corporate version of the good old days Doordarshan Ad on female feticide awareness campaign.*

The bias doesn't end here. It continues to bug once a female candidate gets a job. Working as a colleague is a different thing and accepting them as a line manager is different. We still haven't graduated to take up commands from female bosses.

There are many examples I have seen with the female co-workers where people become opinionated about a female line manager. Many times, I hear from people about the reaction they have got from their female LM. When probed with example, if this is not a similar response you had got when you had a male LM, people tend to change the topic, but not their opinion. I have examples of ladies working with us who either compromised with the situation and accepted things with a "pinch of salt" or became loud and moved towards judgmental acceptance of the situation out of frustration.

Perhaps we are programmed to think patriarchally.

It would take time for us as society to accept the existence of females in our workplace, valuing them perhaps would take even more time. We would take time to understand that accomplishment of tasks/goals accomplishment is important,than the physical appearance or gender.

We as individuals may bring a bigger shift in this. If not in the current generation, we can train the next generation by setting a good example. The #breakthebias could happen only when it starts from our homes. The moment we have better discussions in the house and can give independence to the female of the house in taking bigger decisions, without prying, it would kind of set pressure on our kids to accept this (my patriarchal upbringing influenced me to write this using the word "Independence"). The decision should be beyond "what to cook" and "who will wear what".

#breakthebias trend I feel is the corporate version of the good old days' Doordarshan Ad on female feticide awareness campaign.

So next time when you are getting opinionated about any female around you, based the work or otherwise, ask yourself, **"When was the last time you took effort to break the bias at your home?"**.

EXPERIENTIAL BIASNESS AND THE IRON CURTAIN

When was the last time you tried removing the Iron Curtain from your mind?.

Most of us are driven by our firsthand experiences. When we learn from our own experiences, we kind of start believing that the knowledge gained during the experiences is earned knowledge and, to all the probability, is the best learning one can have in such situations. But the problem arises when these experiences bring bias in our thoughts and actions. This starts making an Iron Curtain that get pulled over our thoughts and vision. We get so driven by our own experiential bias that we stop thinking of solutions beyond our experiential learning. We start believing that the iron curtain that is drawn over our thoughts is the impervious wall we had made to handle the situation and can't be removed.

After all, we have earned our experiences, and the iron curtain is being interlaced by us only, basis our bias towards our firsthand learning experiences.

> The experiential biasness starts making an Iron Curtain that get pulled over our thoughts and vision.

I was talking to one of our business partners and was discussing improving his ROI. I had suggested some corrective actions to him. He acknowledged that these actions would help him improve upon his earnings and the overall health of the business. But the problem came when we started discussing the timelines to implement what we discussed to improve his organization's business health. His experiential bias started playing a significant role and he was too apprehensive about the repercussions of these actions. He had an opinion that the place he is in is a small-town where people with limited thought process and exposure to new learning. Any such actions would not be welcome by the trade. He was having a fear of losing the business and thought that it's better to live with a thin ROI than getting into a situation not welcomed by the trade.

We often come into such a situation that could lead to delaying the entire process just because of our own experiential bias. We fear taking steps that we know are right but have less confidence that it will work.

> Being open to evaluate our learning and ready to top up our learning to match with the changing needs may help us to be relevant in the current times.

There many such examples are there where people have shown resistance to try something new out of the same experiential bias. This is a very common phenomenon where the majority are driven by their bias. Those who try are the one who wins over them.

I think **being open to evaluating our learning** from certain experiences would help us get away from any such bias. Some of the steps could be considered bold at a certain point in time, but if we are confident enough in the risk we are taking and if we have calculated the risk, it is still worth taking those calls.

It is important to remove those Iron Curtains that we had drawn in front of us basis our own experiences and be open enough to avoid related bias.

If the iron curtain is not removed, trust me, we will miss the opportunity of learning something new, doing better and reaping better.

If these iron curtains are not removed, we will become obsolete over a period of time. People with this perpetual Iron Curtains are majority in number around and these are the average population that are always driven by the "in our days" phrase and never try to take new learning or processes easily.

So, next time when you are in a conflicting situation of your own earned learning and others', earned learning, ask yourself, **"When was the last time you tried removing the Iron Curtain from your mind?"**

GENERATION GAP

When was the last time you were considerate with the changing needs of the new generation?

Dad, you may not understand us. Perhaps a gap in our thought process is there, maybe a generation gap..."

I never thought that I would have to get into this conversation sometime and be on the receiving end.

The discussion started with naming generation, Gen X, Gen Y, Millennial, Bloomers, Gen Z, Gen Alpha, and progressed to the thought process of each generation to the ways of seeing career to the gender views, to the ways of seeing relationship. This further moved towards identifying each other during the conversation as to which generation we belong to. Basically, understanding the traits of each generation.

The discussion proceeded towards the relationship and each generation's views of seeing it. I realised that I belong to that so-called "old school" thought where a vision is inherited rather than developed, as perceived by this brand-new generation.

> *The new generation always blame the previous generation as inheriting the vision than developing with experience.*

While in discussion when I said that this is quite a Western way of seeing relationships, and I call it the Hippie way, which is now diminishing in the Western world as well. The "new generation" people felt offended by hearing this, and I got a pushback on labelling them for following Western thoughts. They said if you do not agree with anything of our generation, you put it to the western world and start blaming us for copying them. However, there is no problem in saying so, but you do not want us to develop thoughts that do not suit you. That's the problem of your generation. There is a generation gap between us, and you will never understand us.

I generally keep my accommodating hat handy and take it out when required. To accommodate here, I immediately said, "Let's be happy with each other's thoughts. There is no point discussing something we never develop consensus upon, especially when it starts with Ours and Yours, as we would never agree upon some of the thoughts."

> *The easy way to get mingled with new generation is having a non-judgemental ear while listening to them.*

Without being judgmental about this Gen Z's thoughts, I think somewhere we need to let our new people develop their thoughts, even if we know they are wrong. Let them understand by making mistakes. But standing strong for them is required to hold them from falling, like our father did.

This Gen Z thing is even more fierce in a corporate environment. The span of concentration and the patience of this generation are a bit thin. This doesn't mean that the efficiency of this generation is also low. This is a better and learned generation. The only issue is they need more space everywhere, and it at times leads to compromising with the work, and even the urgency of work at times takes a back seat.

> *New generation has their own ways of communicating with each other; even emoji is a language for them.*

My experience with this generation has been better, where I was able to take the best from them. The one thing this generation values the most is communication and knows to communicate better than others. They have their ways of seeing communication. To them, the communication is not always about talking to each other in volume or getting into too much of the details when a context setting is not required. So, taking a cue out of it, I have always been a good listener to them, and this itself was the biggest gap solver for me. Many times, this generation communicates not necessarily to get the solution, they have one. They communicate just to express and get heard with no intention of getting empathy in exchange. This generation at times uses emojis to communicate, which might be difficult to comprehend by us, but we need to learn this. An emoji way of communication might look absurd to us, but that's the way the new generation expresses their feelings and understands others.

Out of all these, my only worry is that the way mental well-being is spoken about, and the way cases of mental health is rising, we as a society need to let our new generation raise patiently, both personally and professionally. Even if we hate getting labelled as old school people. After all we were rebels during our time.

So next time if you get irritated with the thought of the new generation, ask yourself **"When was the last time you were considerate with the changing needs of the new generation?"**

HAVE YOU CELEBRATED YOUR FAILURE?

Have you celebrated your failures and mistake?

It sounds weary, but the fact of life is, no one teaches us better than our mistakes and failures. It is not easy to accept failure. Many times, we feel dejected and at times go into a shell and tend to disconnect ourselves. A failure brings a shift in the mental status of many and sees this as a defeat for themselves. But each failure is a stepping stone towards success. So, more than accepting the failure, it is important to show resilience. The time taken to rebound from it decides the long-term fate for a person. The sooner we can understand, the faster we can bring success to us.

Once, while checking in for the hotel in Goa, I saw a pilot waiting for his turn to check in at the reception of the hotel. Since I was also waiting, I thought of talking to him. We spoke for a while and I wanted to understand a situation, so I asked the pilot, "Captain, while driving the car, we often make mistakes, like not slowing down when a speed breaker is there, or at times getting into another lane without blinking. I am sure you guys must be making these silly mistakes while flying an aircraft. How do you handle that?"

The captain smiled and said, "While we are trained to make fewer mistakes, we do make mistakes while flying. As long as we know how to manoeuvre the situation, we can control everything without even letting the passengers know."

Scary, but some of the good learning in the discussion was getting trained to make fewer mistakes, which means they learn these during their simulation exercises. The other point to remember was knowing the ways of manoeuvring around the mistakes. Most importantly, if we are handling the situation, it is required to be calm and not let the business get affected and transfer the worry to the customers.

We often hear that the one who is successful is the one who makes fewer mistakes. I think a successful person has made enough mistakes in their early times that (s)he now has good cases to differentiate and understand what could lead to failure and hence should not take that. A point to contemplate here is, today's successful people are the one who made mistakes in the past. Even now, they would be making mistakes and seeing failure. But they have mastered the art of rebounding.

> *Each failure is the stepping stone towards a bigger success.*

But the question is, how can we manage the stress that comes with the mistakes and failures?

There is no set formula for this. For me, the easiest way is to accept the failures and understand the mistakes that we made while taking up the task. Taking the failure or mistakes to heart will not solve the issues; in fact, it would complicate by reducing our self-esteem.

I strongly believe in the fact that we should allow people to make mistakes and let them taste failure. This actually would help him/her learn faster. It is important to ensure each mistake gives us some learning and helps us understand what not to repeat again.

> *Celebrate a failure with "Coffee & Me" moment to retrospect and understand what went wrong.*

But above all, what is vital is to celebrate our mistakes and failures. If not much, just treat yourselves with a cup of good coffee every time you make a mistake. And while treating yourselves with a cup of coffee, have it alone since it's your own mistake. Utilize that "Coffee and Me" time to evaluate what went wrong and what could have been sidestepped to make it a success. What are the learnings from the mistakes you have made? What should be kept in mind next time we are taking such or related work to avoid further failures? This would do wonders for you.

We have read many stories of failure and resilience during our school and college days. One that most of us remember is of Edison. While inventing the light bulb, he had seen many failures. But he never stopped making mistakes and giving up the idea of inventing a bulb. When he finally succeeded, someone asked him about his experiences. Edison mentioned that he now knows 999 different ways of how to not make a bulb. This is one of the best examples of showing resilience and enjoying the journey failure to success.

We all must have fallen down many times while learning to cycle during our childhood days. Have those deterred us from learning the cycle? Every time we were falling, we were learning what can make us fall. Even if we had bruised elbows or knees, we never gave up the idea of learning how to ride a bicycle. We all must remember the joy of covering a distance for the first time without falling. That is the joy of success and is priceless.

So, the next time when a failure gives you stress, ask yourself, **"When Was the Last Time You Celebrated Your Failure?"**.

NOSTALGIA MOMENT

When was the last time you worked to create your nostalgia for future?

Whenever old co-workers meet, one very common topic of discussion is the stories that were there when they were working together. Most of the time, it's the discussion about the nostalgia that they all or one of them has created.

Those nostalgic moments could be anything, spanning from great achievements to the great processes to achieve the goal, or just the happy moments. Mostly these moments of discussion are the ones that have brought success, joy, or just a fun moment.

> Talking to old colleague and travelling down memory lane always gives nostalgic experience.

All agree upon their self-established fact of being the best team of their time, and perhaps re-creating that time and team is not easy. All that it speaks in length is the happiness that was there during their time. There were tough situations, but they had never missed the chance of celebrating and had been very well connected, supporting each other during their individual tough times to succeed as a team.

This will not be understood by someone who has just started their career. But if you have experience working in different organizations or teams, you will definitely agree that travelling down memory lane with someone we share that time is always nostalgic.

Putting this to the current context, we must work every day in a way that we are creating a nostalgic moment for the future. Use the communication to ensure we are connected, learn from each other, work for ourselves but chase the goal as a team, support each other by either pushing to achieve big or shouldering some of the responsibilities of a teammate if they are in some troubling situation. This will lead to not only a happy now but also will give you enough content to feel happy about 5 – 10 years from now, when the old team members sit together and remember old times.

Working everyday as if we are creating nostalgic moment for future will help reducing today's stress.

This is not easy. But neither difficult. Being a team player will make it easy. Many times, we come across some of the team members who tend to be so self-centred that they give a notion of dissociation with the team. Not that they do not do good, but they do good for only themselves. This slowly starts giving stress to the team members, and that team member would easily become a talk among others, and may get hated by the other team members.

It is the responsibility of the team leader to ensure better communication within the team and must work as One Team. This will not only help reducing the stress within the team but also would help team create those nostalgic moments for future.

So, next time when you are working in a team, ask yourself, **"When was the last time you worked to create your nostalgia for future?"**

THE OBVIOUS IS INVISIBLE

When was the last time you did not observe the obvious?

It was a good bright afternoon when I had my lunch at the office and came down with one of my colleagues to take a post lunch walk before getting into work again. There is a designated smoking area at one corner of the open space downstair. My colleague wanted to have a fag and so I accompanied him there. He was smoking and we were involved in some discussion that we stopped only when a person came to me and asked for a lighter... I was not smoking, my colleague was smoking, this person came to me and asked for a lighter... I mean is it not obvious that the one who is smoking should have a higher probability of having a lighter than the one who is not. How can someone be that ignorant that he/she cannot see the obvious and could rather look for the solution in something which is not even visible.

Most of the time, obvious are always invisible.

This was one of a kind of incident. But if we look around, we can see many such stories and instances. I think the obvious is always invisible. So invisible that people tend to ignore it.

This oblivious situation is witnessed everywhere, be it in personal life or professional life.

I too have got into many such situations in the past and even at times, these days. I am sure this is the experience of most of us. Have we not observed a situation when someone is badly searching for something, and some other pitch in, to let them understand that it was right there where they were searching, or the solution was there with them that they practiced upon many times in past. A similar situation must have happened with all of us every day or sometimes.

In professional life when in some crisis situation, we keep getting into too much analysis and the answer most of the time is pretty simple, that were ignored by us while into the evaluation process. It is fancy to look for a complex solution than acknowledging a simple one.

This is one form of absent-mindedness that we are infected with at times. It is required in such a situation to maintain our cool and ensure not rushing into the decision by taking steps that give a deceptive look at being the solution but actually are the short-term fix.

> *Crisis situation most often leads to getting into too much of analysis paralysis.*

The best way to avoid such a situation is not to get in a hurry of finding the solution. We must first split the case into steps to understand where the problem is. Fishbone is one very strong tool to do so. Now for each of the steps, identify if the problem is there in that step or not. Do not always get into too much analysis paralysis initially and use our common sense, by reducing the absent mindedness. Once we are able to understand which step is having the issue or where the problem lies, look for the solution that is very specific to that step. The solution could be the easiest one that was being ignored. For all the situation or problem, not necessarily the solution is the toughest one. The solution could be right there that was being ignored. I always believe in the fact that it is better to go back to the basics and refer from there to find the desired solution.

The solution could be the obvious one.

So next time you are looking into some complex situation and scratching your head to find the solution, ask yourself, **"When was the last time you have not observed the obvious?"**

OLD NEWSPAPER

When was the last time you read an old newspaper to know the current news?

All through our career, we always work to deliver and be counted. And if we lead the KPI and always be on top in the ranking, nothing is more soul satisfying than this.

As it is always said that the one at the top will have to keep working hard, more than the one at the lesser rank since losing the position is much easier than gaining one. But the obstruse situation comes when we continue to be at the top and then suddenly drops from there. There could be multiple reasons for that but in most cases, the reason could be performance fatigue.

> *Being on top for some time leads to mental inertia and brings performance fatigue in us.*

It's the relative motion theory where if we have a couple of good years, we start believing that things are settled now, and we slow down on our efforts considering it to be a rolling wheel. We get into a comfort zone and start believing that the place belongs to and remain with us, even if we do not make any efforts. But like any rolling wheel, if we do not keep pushing it, the wheel would start slowing down and would stop traveling after some distance.

Once, I conducted a larger team meeting post COVID era. During the COVID, our product demand grew multifold and literally, we were increasing sales while sitting at home. It was a natural demand that had been generated for our products. This had brought complacency among the team, and everyone had great sales numbers and success stories of that era. Post-COVID, when the economy was taking a different turn, we ended up sitting at a high base with a bit reduced demand. The team was having past laurels to drool upon, and complacency had started overshadowing their efficiency. I had a task to break that inertia among the team. So, before the team could take their seats in the meeting hall, I asked hotel officials to keep a few old newspapers on each table. When the entire team took their seats, they were a bit surprised to see newspapers on each table since usually we keep a writing pad and pencil there on the table.

I started with a welcome note at the meeting. After the welcome note, I asked each table guy to read "Today's" news that they feel is most important news from the newspaper. Some of the guys raised their hands and started reading the news that for him was important. While reading, they suddenly realized that they are reading old news. Some of them then stared upon the date in the newspaper and realized that they were reading old newspapers. I heard a single loud sound from most of them saying we cannot find new news in old newspapers.

That was a winning moment for me since that is what I wanted them to say. I started building upon this and connected that with the COVID era sales. Yes, we all had our own pieces of success stories during COVID time, but time has changed. Why are we still reading that old newspaper now? We need to start writing new stories and new news to further build than keep staying in the past laurels.

This exercise had blown away their complacency, and each of the meeting attendees understood the message. This helped me to drive innovation in sales from them, and many had improved upon their performance as well.

Getting away from this is not easy. We keep brooding upon past laurels. We forget in the process that old newspapers can be used for reference, impetus, and pride, but definitely not for new news. No one wants to read old news daily.

You must have come across people who created glories in the past, and feel that all that they did in the past can be replicated using the same steps that they took during that time. We need to understand that if something is not science, those steps can only be used for reference purposes and nothing else.

In my personal and professional life, I have seen people living in the past laurels and do not realize that the present time is not being used for creating laurels for the future. This leads to mental inertia and could lead to stagnation in life, be it personal or professional. Living in the past will not bring bigger successes in the present or future.

Consistency and honest intent will make us relevant.

We need to keep creating new news to keep attracting people's share of thoughts towards us. What wins and surefire wins is consistency and honest intention. A performance fatigue is quite human, but what is important is how fast we get out of that circle and move faster, with more vigor, more flamboyantly.

So, next time, if you feel mental inertia, ask yourself, **"When was the last time you read the old newspaper?"**

OPEN TO HEARING BAD NEWS

When was the last time you were prepared to hear bad news?

All of us like and only like good news. We wish to hear good news only, even if we know we are not in a situation to get one. Perhaps none of us likes or wait for or even like to anticipate hearing bad news.

This is all because of the fact that we train our brain to hear what we wish to hear rather than what could actually happen, the pragmatic view.

> *Manifestation never brings better results, thoughtful and honest action can.*

This is more experienced in the professional environments. When we know what we planned at the start of the project or quarter or month, is not going to get delivered the same way at the end, we still hope not to hear or think of the bad that is going to happen. We still want to believe that towards the end everything will happen as per our plan or wish. This could only lead to postponing the bad news and not necessarily will lead to change in the situation. Manifestation never brings better results, only thoughtful action can. Being pragmatic could lead to lesser mental dent than wish of seeing the happy ending.

I have experienced many such instances when we as a team know that we are not going to hear the better news towards the end of the month, we tend not to hear that and keep pushing away the bad news. In my sales career, in the middle of the month only it is realized that this month is not going to give us the desired deliverables, but we are not ready to hear that. We keep pushing with the hope that this one is the push that was missing for the one that would lead to the results we are looking for. While we all know, nothing is going to change.

Ideally, we must not be too much dissenting and must be rational on the planned aim. If we are very optimistic basis our gut feeler only and not topped up with data and experiences, it would always lead to this error. Being a calculated rebel would be a better idea. Failure or the deviation from the plan could happen, and being prepared to hear bad news is always a better thing. The watch out at that point is reducing the gap between the goal v/s achievement over the axis.

> Being a calculated rebel is always better than enthusiastic martyr.

If you know you are going to get bad news towards the end, you may not change the situation much. However, flagging on time and bringing the team together to identify ways to reduce the gap over the plan could build a better environment. I am particularly not a fan of post facto analysis or postmortem exercises. I prefer being proactive rather than living a lacklustre life.

This is not easy. If we are not accustomed to bite a bullet and always in a manifestation of achieving what is planned, a failure would lead to irritation and push us to be judgmental. The most often judgemental situation arises when we start judging our people, and their intent, on the ground. This would not lead to a better environment in the organization, amounting to increased stress, trust deficit and even increased attrition.

So, next time, if you do not achieve the one planned at the start, ask yourself, **"When was the last time you were prepared to hear bad news?"**

PLAN A, B, C, OR PLAN A1, A2, A3

When was the last time you changed the steps of the plan rather than changing the entire plan?

"What is the Plan B?" Most of us have heard this from our LM or the peer group or someone near us.

With the conspicuousness of data and improved analytics we have, I think the world has stirred towards better decision quality. We have learned from machine learning, and hence we like to split the tasks into multiple steps. The stakeholders for most of these steps are very much demarcated. While ambiguity in the external and even internal environment is quite inevitable and could affect the end output of the tasks, it is required that we have Plan B ready with us. But what is equally important is to have safeguards for each step of our plan also, without deviating from the initial process we had adopted to get the desired output. One confidence required is that while we started conceptualizing, we had considered most aspects of the planning while keeping end results in mind. The major step towards an output is planning it better at the start.

> *With the advent of better data analytics, the world is moving towards improved decision quality.*

If we move to Plan B because Plan A doesn't work, we accept the fact that perhaps Plan A wasn't the plan but just a thought with less groundwork. Or perhaps not much homework was done before drafting Plan A. Or perhaps, the execution was flawed for Plan A.

In general, if we are talking about Plan A, B, C, and so on, we are talking about different strategies or the change in the strategies. But when I am talking about A1, A2, A3, and so on, I am more referring to variations within a strategy.

Changing a strategy to achieve a desired goal in case the initial plan doesn't work could be considered as agility to reduce the heavy financial or confidence loss for the organization.

But doing it often will be a reflection of poor leadership, under which the entire task is being planned.

Let's learn from an example.

Suppose you want to get into product development and are strategizing on that. So here could be possible different strategies or Plan A, B, C: -

Plan A: Plan to develop a product in-house.

Plan B: Outsource development to an external agency or firm.

Plan C: Buy an existing product and rebrand it.

Now, making a choice of each strategy would be having a checklist: -

- My organization has capabilities in terms of experienced manpower who know the product development, and my organization has the necessary tools to support this, I would go ahead with **Plan A**.
- If I feel that we are not fitting into the above, or we have too much on our plate that we need to add more manpower to initiate the new product development. New manpower recruitment does not fit into our current situation or plans, but new product development is required to improve the PLC; we may opt for **Plan B**.
- If we find an existing product almost near to our conceptualized product and it is possible to rebrand it, considering the required work was not undertaken by the current owners, I will go with **Plan C**.

In the above example, suppose we are going ahead with **Plan A** after taking into consideration all the required checklists, here could be possible Plan A1, A2, A3: -

Plan A1: - Build a prototype

Plan A2: - Conduct test marketing in a controlled environment.

Plan A3: - Launch the product with the core features and distinctive selling stories.

Now, in this example, if any of the Plan A1, A2, or A3 fails, I would not shift to Plan B. Rather would prefer to correct that particular step or change that particular step.

We need to be more effective at the planning stage of any job given and required to split it into smaller tasks and should have some back up plan also ready for almost every critical step to make it Plan A1, Plan A2 and so on. We do have to take into consideration Plan B as well, following a similar process to that of Plan A, to ensure the initial planned output. However, we should take Plan B only if we anticipate the lesser success of the initial plan or Plan A. But in the maximum possible way we should avoid changing the plan as this would cost the organization time and money.

> Changing the entire plan than steps would cost the organization time, money and would lead to opportunity loss.

While doing all this, I think, going conventional is also not to be left abandoned. With all the data / information, we might have made a certain plan but could go completely wrong in due course of implementation stage. We need to be open to learning and should record these failures in some way to ensure this would give path to others or could be considered as reference or case study for others.

So, the next time if you think a certain plan is not working and need to move to backup plan, ask yourself **"When was the last time you changed the steps of the plan rather than changing the entire plan"**?

TEACHING FISH TO CLIMB

When was the last time you sincerely taught a fish to climb a tree?

Everybody is a genius in their own way. But if you judge a fish by its ability to climb a tree, it will live its whole life believing that it is stupid. This is said to be the statement made by the great Albert Einstein.

This is one of the most-used phrases in the corporate world. So common that almost every one of us must have heard this from our bosses or peer group.

The phrase is used to mention that each one has their intrinsic characteristics and is unique from others. If people with different capabilities are given work from the other set where there is no match with their capabilities, not even close to their capabilities, there is a high probability of failure. This phrase is used mainly to let the leaders understand that they should be good enough to understand the ability of their team members and assign the work according to their ability to get the maximum out of it. It is all about identifying the right fit for the candidates and team members.

> *At times, a leader becomes premeditated about teaching the art of climbing to the fish that they start taking failure of the fish to climb the tree, as their failure.*

New leaders often make mistakes by addressing their own desire rather than the ability of their team members. They keep pushing people beyond their ability to get things done. The bigger problem arises when out of enthusiasm, these leaders start measuring their leadership basis their ability to teach a fish to climb. At times, they become so very premeditated about teaching the art of climbing to the fish that they start taking the failure of the fish to climb the tree as their failure.

In one of the instances in my leadership role to a new geo, my LM once told me to take a call with one of my team members as he had an understanding that she was less capable and was a bottleneck in the system. I resisted and told my LM to give me some time to form an opinion. I generally believe in getting firsthand experiences when the relevant data is not quite satisfying to me. This was one such case where the logic of my LM to take the call over the associate was not convincing enough for me. Since my LM had a certain amount of confidence in me and my decision making, he agreed upon the time and gave me confidence in going ahead with my judgment in this matter.

While working with her, I realized that she has got capabilities in some different areas, and the issue is with the job assigned to her. She was one of the cases of accessing the fish based on her skill to climb the tree.

Somehow, I managed to convince my LM to assign her a job she could be good with than showing her the exit gate. She got transferred to different departments and did extremely well there and proved to be one of the most valued employees of the organization. It's all about the right fitment in this case. A fish has been given an ocean to swim than a tree to climb.

> *Mapping the capability of team helps a leader to take decision on their right fitment for the job.*

When we start handling a new team, it is strongly recommended to map the competence of each team member to understand their capabilities and their fitment in the role. There could be a possibility that some may not be the right fitment itself, and you may not get the opportunity to place them anywhere within the organization based on the capability. It is advisable to let them go in such cases. This will be good for them as well, since staying in the wrong job may lead to mental stress and may cause a loss of confidence. This is another problem with many of the new-age Line Managers. They tend to hate the attrition and often feel offended about it. But we need to understand one thing that when your ocean does not have space to swim for a fish, you need to let them go to swim in another ocean than keep adjusting with the current situation by letting them try new trees to learn the art of climbing, for the name of being a people leader, the most misunderstood phrase.

Once capabilities are mapped, involve them in their kind of job. If you see possibilities of upgrading them based on the requirements of the current job, put efforts into improving them. Recommend them for the right set of workshops, within or outside the organization. This will help them be well-equipped and will help the organization in the long run. This will also help you upgrade to a leader from the manager.

Upgrading team members on their capability is the prime responsibility of the LM and is a non-negotiable deed.

Many successful leaders are ones who know the capabilities of their team and utilize their strengths for building the business and value, while simultaneously working on upgrading their team. A successful leader never wastes time on teaching a fish to climb a tree. They would rather look for the right opportunities for themselves and bring the job fitment.

So next time, if you feel failed in your efforts towards upgrading your team member, ask yourself, **"When was the last time you wasted time in teaching a fish to climb the tree?"**

TEMPORARY PROBLEM, PERMANENT SOLUTION

When was the last time you suggested a permanent solution for a temporary problem?

Most of the time, we hear that employees do not leave a company; they often leave a boss. And we strappingly believe it as well. Really… I think this is one best examples of giving a permanent solution to a very temporary problem. This is one illogical solution heard most often. I mean, and we really think that the guy left the organization because of boss could have stayed with us to build my organization. With this decision quality, are we sure organization can be built?

> *Leaving an organization because of LM, is one such case of permanent solution for a temporary problem.*

Amidst we put our energy justifying why my Line Manager is inefficient – freeloading - dumb, we could have routed our energy to have an active discussion with him/her on what better we can do in the conflicting situation. We can route our energy towards understanding what is going wrong and why there is a misalignment or conflict happening with the Line Manager. We can even have active communication on finding a ground amicable to both, and that could lead to working towards the organization's goal in a more efficient way.

Leaving an organization because my Line Manager is inefficient is more like raising questions on the organization's process of promoting talent. An act of proving the point that I am right, and the boss, organization, and processes are wrong. This is not necessarily the case always. Getting promoted without capability is a less common occurrence in any organization. What possibly makes one the right fit or wrong fit as a boss is his/her ability to be open to new learning.

A line manager is the most temporary entity in the team, like any of the team members. LM in a team generally has a span of 2 – 4 years. So, the one who is the influencing factor of taking a permanent solution himself has a temporary tenure. If the organization is good enough and you are seeing your future, there is no point in thinking of taking a call to give a permanent solution to a very temporary problem.

Conflict with LM could be resolved by having an active communication with a non-judgmental mindset.

When such issues arise, it is always encouraged to see things differently and try building a common ground in the team to lead an amicable relationship that is fulfilling not only for us but also leading to better efficiency. This will benefit all and will bring a Win-Win situation within the organization. Active communication is encouraged with a non-judgmental mindset.

Not every problem requires a grand or path-breaking solution. Sometimes it's better to observe and understand before acting.

So, next time if you are thinking of leaving an organization because of the Line Manager, ask yourself, **"When was the last time you suggested a permanent solution for a temporary problem?"**

TO READ IS TO WRITE

When was the last time you recalled what you read in your favourite book five years ago?

Reading has always been a hobby of mine that turned into passion. I don't know when I opted for this and who influenced me to read but I was always looking for an opportunity to get new books to read. Initially these book reading was mainly through borrowing or getting one from the library near me or from my school and college library.

When I became a bit able, I started developing this hobby and in due course have built a good personal library with more than 500 books, almost all read by me. The books are getting added even now in my personal library. Though the only change that has happened is the time spent on reading. It is getting reduced due to other engagements and work. However, I still try my best to take time out to read and have not fixed any time for reading. I read whenever I get any spare time, I read whenever I feel like reading, I read when there is no spare time and, I genuinely want to read and take time out of whatever

I am into. These days, I am having many work-related travels and that's when I read the most.

> *Reading always brings more confidence to anyone as this enables them with the authentic content.*

Reading is one of the best addictions anyone can have. This not only enables you with the correct knowledge but also makes you more confident. This is more relevant in current situations as well as nowadays, the knowledge is quite borrowed and is incomplete with the people. That is one very dangerous thing to have.

During my MBA days, I had come across a book in our college library, called "Kaizen", beautifully written, though I forgot the author's name. The book was so interesting that I finished this in just three sittings. Some of the learning is still there with me, if not all. The Kaizen principle is used mostly by the business houses, but is relevant in our everyday life as well, if embraced well.

Around 16 years after reading that book, I thought of reading it again. Unfortunately, it took time to find that book. Somehow got one written by Sarah Harvey. I had faded memories of the one I read during my college days, so I found this book interesting too. While reading, one thing I realized was that reading books is an art and not everyone master that. To revisit this concept of Kaizen, I had to read this entire book, which I had already read once, it took me a little more than 3 sitting to finish, however, this time.

So, what's the best way to read? I think the best way to read is to write. Meaning if I read a book, after finishing the book or perhaps a chapter of it, I should write a one-page summary or my interpretation of that chapter or book. This will help me have a mini version of that book which I can any time revisit without spending much time. It could be a ready reckoner of the book. This would help understand the book better as well since writing what you read could take the learning of the book a bit more deeply rooted in our mind and memory. Besides, this would help us have more content to talk about and refer to when needed in the conversation.

> *Writing a summary of the book read helps us create our own vault of learning that can be a ready reckoner for us.*

I do that often now, and my one-page vault is growing. It's not a kind of second copy of the book I read, but more of the paragraphs or bulleted points that act as a summary of that book. Now feel more confident and can easily recall a book I read. This, at the same time, is available for reference as and when we require this.

So next time, when you feel like reading a book today, ask yourself, **"When was the last time you recalled what you read five years back?"**

YOUR SHOE MY SHOE

When was the last time you tried fitting into a shoe you left wearing a few years back?

"You won't understand what I am going through! You can't feel the pain of wearing the shoes I am wearing unless you put your feet into my shoes."

A very common argument, or rather emotional statement, we hear when we try to nag someone.

This is a very common statement in official space. But what really kind of beyond my understanding is, "Why should I wear your shoes? Do you think I reached here barefoot? Why do you think that I have not experienced such a situation as you are going through? But I haven't complained, rather I ensured to overcome the pain of that nasty pricking and move on than complaining about the situation".

> *In the name of empathy, many managers tend to wear the shoes of the fellow team members that is one act of discouraging the development of the team members.*

Most often, a line manager makes the mistake of feeling the pain and developing empathy towards their report. By doing this, the manager thinks that he is being a better team player and people leader. I think we in this way are actually weakening the desire to acquire strength by the associate. In the process of becoming a leader, we fall into the trap of producing followers rather than begetting leaders. The manager can put his feet into their shoes and can navigate the situation better than them since he has once worn those shoes.

We can coach them to navigate, encourage team members to think about the possible reasons and solutions of the situation, help them in introspecting and retrospection, and develop them to come out of this, unless the situation is worsened to the level that higher-ups intervention is required.

> *We must coach a team manager to become team leader.*

We have often seen teams that do not perform well. Performance could be affected by multiple factors, some may be under control, and some are beyond internal control. But in any case, the team navigates such situations and shows some spark towards achieving the task, plan, or the given goal. The team that struggles is the team where the shoes are shared among the leader of the team and the team members. The best way to deal with such situations is not to be judgmental about the entire team, but to train the leader of the team. Training the leaders to do what is expected of them and not behave like their team members. He graduated from that level and is going back to the old days' experiences wearing old shoes is very unnecessary.

A leader begets leader.

What perhaps is discouraged to do is for LM to wear that shoe and start giving solutions. This happens mostly when an LM is promoted recently. Or in cases where the manager misunderstands the meaning of being a people leader and ways of becoming so. In most cases, they take time to leave the old shoes and put efforts to fit into the new ones. Wise is, the sooner we adjust to the new one, the better it will help build enabled people and professionals in the team.

A people leader is someone who inspires, supports, and uplifts team members than just directing them to achieve the goal. While empathy is one key precursor for the people leader, what they focus more upon is empowering the team and building a growth mindset among them.

An enabled team can navigate the complex situation much more easily. The moment a team learns to encourage each other to be a solution provider than shoe sharing, the team collectively becomes a winning team. The team would be proud of it.

So next time when things are going haywire in your team, ask yourself, **"When was the last time you tried fitting into a shoe you left wearing a few years back?"**

FIRST TIME

When was the last time you did something for the first time?

This is a very interesting phrase I heard some time back. This phrase itself sounds to me like a complete book. I can write a whole book on that. This phrase has literally opened all the examples in my memory lane.

People are resistant to change and always give pushback to it in a quest to avoid any change. The simple reason for this is, any change pushes us to deviate from our ways of working that we are now used to. But change is inevitable. We cannot avoid it by any chance. Embracing change is the best way to be relevant in a changing environment.

> *People by nature are resistant to change in a fear of losing the inertia.*

Around two decades back, the organization I was working for had initiated its digitization journey. While it was a first-time thing even for me and many people like me, we were facing solid resistance from the team and distributors towards this. Until then, we were doing all the claiming, order booking, billing, etc, manually. By embracing digitization, we all have benefited in reducing the manual work, which is time-consuming, error reduction, as machines cannot make any mistakes, getting more authentic data, which can be used for better analytical decision making. Most of the people in the business knew all the benefits of digitization but were having a fear that this would reduce their independence in doing business "their way". Besides, the business will be visible to all in the system and would lead to further complications in the future. In a way, people were thinking that this would become their master and make them slaves of the system. It took us time to establish the digitization footprint among the trade and stabilize this entire piece. This has brought ease of doing business to the business partner as well, to an extent that they started pressuring the team for resolving any technical issues that they faced while working upon the system. But at the start, we faced the challenges on launching this with the relevant stakeholders.

This is one of the examples on the professional front. Many such examples are there around us where people avoid doing anything new in fear of either change in their inertia or failure or larger visibility that could be unsought by the stakeholders.

> *Embracing change will always keep us relevant. Never shy away from doing something for the first time.*

We all must embrace change and keep doing new things to progress. There was a time when Homo Sapiens were living in the caves, having a wild living. But there were few among them who opted to take things for the first time, and over the years has put us in the situation where we are today. So ancestrally we are accustomed to doing it for the first time and embracing changes.

Now the question arises, how to embrace change or reduce friction among people for doing something for the first time. Here is my take on this.

To avoid any resistance to opting for something for the first time, would suggest first listing down all the concerns of doing something for the first time or accepting change. Try getting all the answers from the right person on the concerns listed, understand how this is going to bring better efficiency in the future, and would bring better results for them. Most importantly, ownership of the change will happen only when we can establish that this is the need of the hour, and if not accepted, can lead to being obsolete over time, and that time is also approaching fast. This will help bring a better environment for us to try something new.

Remember, if you are trying something for the first time and are having trust in that, this would bring a better outcome compared to the current status and will help us be future ready.

So, next time when you are resistant to any change and think it's better to continue the way you are doing things, ask yourself, **"When was the last time you did something for the first time?"**

SMALL WINS

When was the last time you celebrated the small wins?

Winning is the most desired thing any individual looks for, everywhere, every day. Winning has always been associated with a connotation of something big that is fulfilling and desired by the team or an individual. Not all achievements qualify to be winning for us as per our set standards in mind.

> *We need to change our perspective towards the winning and be open for identifying small wins.*

In the pursuit of big goals, it's easy to overlook the importance of small victories. While it is important to rejoice every win, we tend not to get kicked upon smaller wins. Small victories are the precursor to the big one. Small wins – a modest incremental achievement can create powerful momentum and significantly enhance the confidence and performance of the individual or a team or the organization.

Small wins are manageable steps that move you closer to larger goals and larger wins. These are specific, actionable, and often measurable. Most importantly, if taken well, it could give a better push to the team to celebrate, be together, and analyse to reach bigger wins.

A small win reinforces our belief that change is possible and sustainable, creating a positive feedback loop of achievement and confidence.

A small win could be anything, like achieving a step of the bigger goal, cracking a tough customer, inching a step ahead versus last month, being a little more productive than last day, or achieving an incentive every month.

On the personal front, small wins can be starting with a 100-meter sprint and adding 100 meter every week to prepare for the marathon run. Every 100 meters you are adding into your sprint is that small win that is going to prepare you for a big marathon.

I generally conduct a virtual meeting with the entire extended team every month over a small victory discussion. I called it "Pratyay – meaning Suffix," stating that every work should have a Suffix of winning. I remember when I started this meeting, in the first meeting, it was really difficult for the team to speak up and share their small victories of that month. We hardly had 3 – 4 stories in a group of 40 people, that too after too much nagging, they could be able to identify them. But slowly team started identifying their winning moments and started waiting for the meeting to share that. A time came when we were having more such stories than the hours slotted for the meeting. This not only has made an impact on the team's confidence but also their morale has lifted. This helped us improve the overall productivity of the team.

> *Celebrating small wins can boost our moral and confidence.*

Leveraging smaller wins is important, and creating moments for the team to achieve small wins could be defined with a simple 5-step process: -

1. Breaking goals into smaller steps
2. Tracking progress towards each step
3. Celebrating as a team the achievement of each step
4. Bringing consistency for the rest of the step
5. Bringing the team together post-achievement of the larger goals to have a bigger celebration.

Small wins may seem insignificant in isolation, but their collective effect is transformative. They build confidence, establish discipline, and give a desire to achieve big.

> Big victories are often built on a foundation of small wins.

Another important thing is celebrating the win by giving ourselves a treat at the end of the achievement. Not necessarily recognition from others can motivate us, even if we can give ourselves a pat on our back by having a me time for the winning celebration.

Small wins are the seed that, if watered properly, can bring big success. Having an eye to understand that small wins are equally important and require our honest evaluation to differentiate between wins and just a process. Big success is often built on a foundation of small wins.

So next time you feel dejected and see the big goals far off, ask yourself, **"When was the last time you celebrated small wins?"**

FOLLOW YOUR PASSION

When was the last time you followed your passion?

Each one of us has some likes and dislikes. Few likes may exceed in our desire to scale towards becoming passionate. Passion is a deep emotional connection to a certain activity that energizes us even in the grave times and helps us bring our right senses in tough times. It increases the overall happiness of the individual since passion is something that is very close to someone pursuing that.

> Passion is a deep emotional connection to certain activity that energizes us every time.

In today's time, when the complexity of life is increasing, when mental well-being is much-talked-about topic, it is important to identify our passion and take time out for that. Our passion helps us grow from within.

If you still don't have passion or have not identified one, take time to understand one. It is not easy to identify our passion. It takes self-realization and effort to discover what excites us the most. This is not easy, though. Passion evolves, adapts with the changing time and age we are in. Passion sometimes camouflages. We may feel something is very close to our heart at times, but get bored soon with that. A passion is not something that we necessarily adopt at an early age. It gets adapted over time and changes with the preferences.

Not everyone discovers their passion at their early stage of life. This is absolutely okay. Identification of passion can take time and can grow over time through experience, exposure, and reflection.

It is always advisable to have one. Identify and develop one for yourself. It will bring a better personality for you, can develop discipline, and ignite innovation in you. Practicing your passion is also important to ensure getting the challenging situation, which can bring best out of you and help develop your continuous learning stint.

> *Passion is not a loud roar in you, but a steady flame that need care and attention to keep burning.*

We often make the mistake of assuming that a passion is some art form that we acquire. A passion could be the work that you are in. If we are passionate about what we are doing, that can also be a drive for us. The only watch out in that is a balancing act. Passion to work should not take away your family time. Passion is helpful in bringing resilience for us, not madness in us. It is not a loud roar in you, but a steady flame that needs care and attention to keep burning.

A passion can be to learn and practice any musical instrument, painting, photography, blogging, writing, pottery, making some electronic devices, programming, playing some games like football or tennis, Gym, designing. The list is endless.

A passion is not required to be unique. A me-too passion is absolutely ok. Passion could be developed naturally in us, or we can get inspired by seeing someone. Getting inspired by someone is not copying someone. Many people can have the same passion and can develop their uniqueness in that.

There are numerous examples where many of the great leader acquires passion beyond the work they are doing. They often talk about their source of energy being their passion to do something that their heart belongs to. They owe some part of their success to their passion.

So, next time when you feel bored and looking for some escape from your regular life, ask yourself, **"When was the last time you followed your passion?"**

END IS THE BEGINNING

When was the last time you started when everything ended?

This is a very strong life lesson. We kept hearing this during our childhood days that there are 7 lives in the Sanatana thought process. The end of one life is the seed to start a new life. We must have read "Antah asti prarambha – अंतः अस्ति प्रारंभः", meaning every end leads to a new start.

This is one of my favourite Sanskrit phrases. This speaks loudly about the importance of resilience, the zeal, and the attitude one must have. While a sunset is the end of a day and signals a nightfall, it also promises a new dawn, a new day to start something fresh and new and find new possibilities for what we may have lost hope last day.

> *Any end is never final, but just a transformation to start something new and better.*

This is also very prevalent in our professional and personal lives. At times, we may feel that it's the end of something, but it actually seeds the start of something new and better. Giving up during that end is actually the end for us. We must not lose hope in any case. Keeping faith on ourselves is very important during those "end times".

We should understand that any end is never a final one but just a transformation point.

It is not easy to maintain our calmness if things are not going well and end very abruptly. During that time, we felt quite helpless and could not understand the ways of coming out of it. We tend to accept this as an end and either compromise with the situation or get into a bit of gloominess. This is the time when we need to keep our patience handy and show our never-give-up attitude. There is always a dawn after a dark night.

> *There is always a difference between an End and Finish.*

What are the ways of getting away from this and living the phrase, end is the beginning. I would suggest a few of the steps that are to be practiced during that time.

1. Take time to come out of this end. I would suggest taking a break and being with yourselves for some time. Utilize this time to do something that you like the most. Cut yourself completely from the end of the

failure that you recently experienced. This will help you come out of this state of mind. This is important, since with a dejected mindset, we cannot create new and better things. A rejuvenation is required to absorb that shock and clear our minds.

2. Evaluate the reasons for the end without attaching emotion to it. Understand what went wrong and what could have been done, given a choice to re-do it. This will give us a learning of what not to do to have an abrupt end to something we are working on.
3. Next is to understand what is next. Say, for example, if we are seeing an end to a project because of some wrong assessments that we made while taking up the project. We now need to understand if anything better that we can identify to intensify the return that may be better than the previous one. Once identified, let's plan better with the right set of actionable steps and a review mechanism to avoid any instance of repeating the mistake.
4. Take the learning at each step and be open to any transformation that is required. A tough decision may be waiting to be made. Be open to that as well.
5. Most importantly, understand that this may also end abruptly. Be agile to take that up very sporadically.

> *Attaching emotion to the end will lead to getting finished.*

No end is penultimate until the end of our breath. There is always a difference between an end and a finish. Understand this and live as if you know how to regenerate.

So next time, when you see everything is getting terminated to an end and you feel nothing is in your hands or within your capacity, take a deep breath and ask yourself, **"When was the last time you started something after it ends?"**

PURPOSE OF LIFE

When was the last time you thought about the purpose of your life?

The business environment is getting more competitive with every passing year. New breeds are coming into the workforce of the world with newer thoughts, new ways of working, and new axes of thinking. But in all these, what is important a question to ask is, why are we doing what we are doing?

> *Having a purpose blended with the work we are in, brings a positive change for all.*

Important is what legacy are we trying to create? How do we want to be remembered? These are questions beyond the day-in-day-out work that we are engaged in.

Finding a purpose for what we are working for is important to create a legacy. The purpose of life for a business professional goes beyond KPIs, the urgent–important matrix, market share that we are working for. It is more about creating value not only for the business and shareholders, but for the society we are in. Having a larger horizon of thought is important.

We must understand that business is a tool mixed with the purpose, creates a magic for society, and acts as a powerful engine for positive change. If we double click this, it will create a bigger value not only for the business that we are engaged in, but also helps us create better equity for ourselves.

We all have come across or heard of great leaders who, at times give a notion of being bigger than the organization. In fact, an organization's equity is the sum total of the leaders working with purpose to bring positive change in the society around.

Finding a purpose in our life while working for an organization can help us make an unforgettable impact and help in our personal growth.

> *The purpose of our life has an impact beyond KPIs we are driving. It is about creating value to the society and being a positive change agent.*

While in a meeting in a boardroom, we often ask or hear the question:

"What's the goal?"

What rarely do we ask or hear is:

"Why does this matter?"

"What impact do we want to make?"

"Whose life will improve by doing this?"

"What legacy do we want to create?"

In a business environment, having a clear purpose is pertinent and much required as this always helps the organization in many better ways than just creating and building numbers.

> *In a business, success is not about "What you earn" but is more about "What you return".*

A purpose-driven organization can **attract more loyal customers**, have **motivated employees**, **foster innovation**, **grow consistently** and **sustainably,** and can be able to **survive downturns**.

In the new age business, success is considered not just in **"What you earn"** but can be defined more by **"What you return"**.

The purpose of life in the business is not only to be successful but also to be impactful. This will always be cherished by all, and the person can have a lasting impact on the business, society, and people. The real ROI in business is not just Return on Investment, but it goes beyond that to Return on Intention.

Find the purpose of life to be more in control of yourself and bring value to the business and yourself. This will help you break the clutter of the new workforce and create value for yourself.

So next time when you feel dejected and struggle to identify why you are doing what you are doing, ask yourself, **"When was the last time you thought about the purpose of life?"**

PROCRASTINATION

When was the last time you avoided procrastination?

Procrastination is a very natural process and a very common phenomenon in everyday life. Sometimes, the procrastination comes without any intent; at times, we get into it involuntarily. Time is not a renewable asset, and once gone is completely lost. It cannot be bought back once lost. This only leaves us with regret.

> *Procrastination is a silent killer of our natural productivity.*

Generally, people procrastinate by spending more time on less urgent or important things. Procrastination could happen by stretching the time on something that we enjoy the most at the cost of something that is a pressing need of the time. At times, this could be one advisable thing to do to get back to our true us, parsimoniously.

Procrastination is still fine for our rejuvenation. But being a habitual procrastinator is one very dangerous thing for us. This could make us extraneous in the environment we are in. Procrastination is a silent killer of our productivity. This could often lead to more stress and can impede our image both in the professional and personal front.

It is important to understand why we procrastinate before getting into remedial actions for this.

Procrastination, according to me, is a state of mind that comes involuntarily to us. When we start thinking too much about some tasks and start evaluating that as, since I am not in the right state of mind, I will do it later, or not relevant to me, or this task belongs to someone else, or not able to prioritize things better, it could lead to procrastination.

This thought is more prevalent when we have high expectations and start fearing failure. In such cases, we start delaying the task with an intent to buy some time to let the expectations mellow down. But unfortunately, if something is important and the critical success factor is decided basis that, mellowing down gets out of context. This actually would lead to pronouncing us towards failure.

> *Low self-discipline is the most important reason of procrastination.*

Lack of motivation could be one of the reasons for this state of mind. When some tasks do not qualify into what I enjoy doing the most, can make me procrastinate. But we need to understand that not everything can fall into our interest level. Some may just be a routine task which could lead to a bigger result and is a critical step towards that. We cannot miss out on that and let it get delayed.

A major reason of developing this state of mind for prolonged hours is low self-discipline.

In today's era, when social media is one of the biggest distractions, instances of procrastination are increasing. The new generation is really into instant gratification, and social media plays where they can easily get quick enjoyment there. I have experienced procrastination cases very rampant with the new generation as they have more distractions in life that is deterring them to take up something that is the most important, and success is decisive upon that.

Chronic procrastination can lead to stress, anxiety, lower productivity, and compromised personal well-being, besides damaging the reputation of an individual.

> *Procrastination is very human; we must understand the trigger for this.*

How to come out of this state of mind is the biggest question now.

Here are a few of the easy steps that we can practice for coming out of procrastination:

1. Large projects or work are often overwhelming. Breaking them into smaller steps with tighter timeline would help us in retaining our interest. Take a controlled break after finishing every step. A Pomodoro technique can help here. In this technique, we can decide to take a break of 25 minutes after finishing every step with being mindful of the actual timeline of the project completion.
2. Being self-disciplined is important for coming out of procrastination. Once we decided the steps and timeline to complete the steps, we must live up to that. Reminding ourselves is important to ensure self-discipline. Self-discipline could come only when we have convinced ourselves on the task and timeline.
3. Limiting the distractions can further help. If we have taken up certain tasks, our major focus should be there. We can reduce the distractions by turning off various notifications, keeping the social media on silent mode. Being mentally available for the work that we are into could help. If some tasks can be done sitting, like finishing an online project, completing a

training module, or data analysis, a quiet place where distractions could be limited is advisable.

4. If the reason for procrastination is fear of failure or self-doubt or maybe over-expectation from us, addressing these psychological conditions is crucial. We should reframe the critical success factor of the project or the task. Getting it aligned with the stakeholders to ensure no unrealistic ask be there is important. In such a situation, self-love is important. Being compassionate and considerate about ourselves is critical.
5. Bringing a state of mind where we should be ready to accept failure. We must understand that the only way to avoid fear of failure is by reframing failure as an opportunity to learn. It's absolutely ok to fail. This should not lead to procrastination. We have already discussed about failure in the previous chapters.

> *Our dreams should be bigger trigger for our work than the short-term enjoyment that is leading to procrastination.*

Another way to handle procrastination is by implementing the Urgent–Important Matrix in our handful of tasks. Here, we should literally be using the chart to list down all our tasks or work that we need to perform. Now place that work in the Urgent - Important Matrix and be intentional about following the timelines basis what we have written in the chart. Self-discipline is again key to this methodology.

Procrastination is human. An introspection can help us with healthy procrastination. By understanding the trigger of procrastination, it will be easier for us to address it. Remember, your dreams are bigger than the short time enjoyment you are getting by procrastinating. We must understand that there are always two ways of seeing the time – I have enough hours with me, or I have just a few hours to finish the task.

So next time when you feel that your state of mind is the biggest reason to waste time, ask yourself, **"When as the last time you avoided procrastination?"**

ROLE MODEL

When was the last time you put in efforts to be a Role Model for someone?

We all have our favourite person whom we like so much that at times we think of becoming like them. This is primarily because we like their conduct, behaviour, action or the way they speak, treat people. We try emulating them or try finding their gumshoe in our personality. We make our own role model out of respect for the person for the principles and ethics that the person follows.

This hero can be a movie star, a teacher, a friend, any family member, or our parents. They make a huge impact on our overall personality development.

> *Role Modelling is one sublet but immensely influential form of silent leadership.*

Role modelling or positive influencing helps organizations reinforce the ethos, drive conscience, boost morale of the people working there, and improve the trust and productivity at an overall level.

Role modelling is one subtle but immensely influential form of silent leadership. This has a bigger impact upon the individual and organization, not only with an interim perspective but also in terms of long-term vision.

While we keep searching for our role model basis our preferences and way of life, there are a lot for whom we could be a role model. Have we given a thought to this? Getting followers basis some of our personality traits is easy, but being a role model is a huge responsibility for us. We must influence people positively with our personality traits. This is a basic obligation of all of us to create a better world and a better future for our next generation. Role modelling is one of the tools towards this.

Now the question is, why is this important?

As discussed, it is a very silent form of leadership that brings a bigger impact upon the individual or teams attached to us. While for us, any specific behaviour is an everyday thing, for others, that could be a talking point. They may be influenced by that behaviour. Over a period, if managed well, Role modelling becomes a habit or behaviour for many.

> Role Modelling is a *full-time job*, and our legitimacy plays a crucial role in this.

Role modelling happens when you start making an impact on someone's life and are helping them grow, personally and professionally.

Being a role model is a big responsibility and must be taken genuinely. While doing role modelling, we must understand that our interests must not be prioritized over the one who are looking upon us. Our legitimacy plays a crucial role in this.

We can practice a few of these pointers for being a role model: -

1. **Being Authentic: -**
   We must be real and authentic. This is one of the basic characteristics everyone likes. We must not be tricky with the people, and our intention should be visible to others. Authenticity should come to us effortlessly, else it will become more theatrics and will be gauged by others. The authenticity can clearly be observed by others in the way we take things up, the way we speak, and the way we deliver what we commit. This is the minimum we expect from our role model, and hence this is the minimum we should be reflecting to be a role model for others.

2. **Practice Transparency: -**
   We should be transparent with our people around us. Concealing information to extract maximum out of

people may one day be understood and may lead to shrinking our face among them. Transparency is the extension of being authentic. Align the team on what we are thinking and what is to be delivered. This may be used by some of the team members in the wrong way, but most would like you to be transparent.

> *A leader begets leader; begetting followers is the politician job.*

3. **Recognize Others: -**
   A true leader is one who always gives credit to the team. Such a leader challenges their team with some of the stretch tasks with a shrinking timeline. He makes people accountable for their domain or task, enabling them to perform it well, but never fails to recognize the team or the individual for doing great job. For them, it is not only the result that matters, but also the steps towards achieving the goal and the efforts taken by the team. Recognition makes the work environment better and develops an appreciative culture that itself acts as a motivation factor for the team. The team in such environments can perform much better and can develop team spirit.

4. **<u>Committed To Growth</u>: -**

   Performance is a behaviour that is inculcated well by the leader. A leader ensures the right commitment to growth by the team. This is not only about the business growth, but a holistic growth of the business, process, environment, and the individual. The leader helps remove all the hurdles to growth, ensuring the commitment of the team does not fall due to these bottlenecks. A leader working continuously towards the growth of the team and ensuring the growth commitment within them can always be perceived as a Role Model.

5. **<u>Enabling People</u>: -**

   It is not about being enabled and acting as a rockstar of the organization but equally important is to ensure enabling people. A leader begets a leader. Begetting a follower is politician's job. A true leader always ensures development of leadership capabilities of the people they are leading. They ensure enabling them to take care of the issues, hurdles, and the vision. Enabled people will always follow the path their leader has suggested and will try to reflect the characteristics of the leader. Role modelling is all about strengthening people to be future ready. This is the impact a role model can make upon their team or the one closely following him/her.

6. **<u>Respect Individuality</u>: -**
   This is about respecting the individuality of the people. We may get tempted to start producing our clones, but what is important is to let the people be they. As a role model, we can just sharpen the edges that we feel is important for the person to be a great leader. For a role model, it is a general tendency that we want more people to be like us, in a way that wants to produce clones. So much so that we sometimes start expecting people to think the way we are thinking. This can reduce the new thought process and new perspectives towards things will start to diminish.

So, next time when you feel blessed to have a role model in your personal or professional life, ask yourself, **"When was the last time you put efforts towards being a role model for someone?".**

LOVE WORK MORE THAN YOURSELF

When was the last time you loved yourself more than your work?

The world today is moving very fast pace. A jostling culture has developed across and is getting glorified. Being a workaholic and productive is the parameter of success and is new measuring unit of self-worth. Long hours of working, sleepless nights, and stacked schedules are no longer considered taboo. We are getting obsessed with success and promotion. But amidst chasing deadlines, we are forgetting the most important investment we'll ever make – investment in ourselves.

The new generation is in much of hurry for success that they are forgetting the importance of health and well-being. We must remember the fact that we are identified by our name and not our designation. A designation is a badge that is never permanent to anyone. The one we are wearing today belonged to someone else yesterday. We never remember a person by their designation they were having but remember by their name and their self-worth.

> *We are recognized by our names and not by the designation we are holding.*

Our work can definitely bring purpose and pride, but can never define our entire existence. We are a social animal and hence have certain societal responsibilities. It is important to love ourselves and recognize that our inner soul does have certain requirements and expectations from us. Our mental wellbeing, relationships, and passion are equally important which differentiate us from other animals.

In the quest for getting success faster, we may start moving towards a burned-out situation. Being burnout is not a feather to be worn as pride. It is a signal our consciousness gives to slow down, take a break, rejuvenate, and move forward. Getting into work fatigue can be lethal and may lead to burnout and hence may start affecting our personal life.

> *A job is just a means to sustain our life, not the reason of our existence.*

We must learn the art of saying "No" to the work when it starts affecting our well-being. Taking a break and giving time to yourself is not a crime, and we must not feel guilty about it.

I always recommend taking a small break at a set frequency from work. During that time, disconnect completely from work and take care of ourselves. This break can be a short break or a longer one to just regain what we lost working. A small walk, getting up early to see the sunrise, or having coffee at our favourite place can also be enough to feel great and feed our inner soul.

The world today is not looking for a workaholic, burned-out mechanical professional. It is in need of happy people who know how to balance their life and can very easily navigate between a happy life and a productive work.

A happy soul can always do magic and will always be in need in a world full of overworked and performance-fatigue individuals.

So next time, when you feel indulging more and more in the work and start feeling being workaholic is a badge of success, ask yourself, **"When was the last time you prioritized and loved yourself more than your work?**

Other Titles by Amitesh

<table>
<tr><td>Kinche
Short Stories collection in Hindi</td><td></td></tr>
<tr><td>Baked Thoughts
Collection of blogs written between 2007 and 2017</td><td></td></tr>
<tr><td>The Adventure of Ricky
The collection of bedtime stories co-authored with his son, Shreeyansh</td><td></td></tr>
<tr><td>Narmada Nandlaal
Short Stories collection in Hindi</td><td></td></tr>
</table>